American Government
CONGRESS

no

D1296036

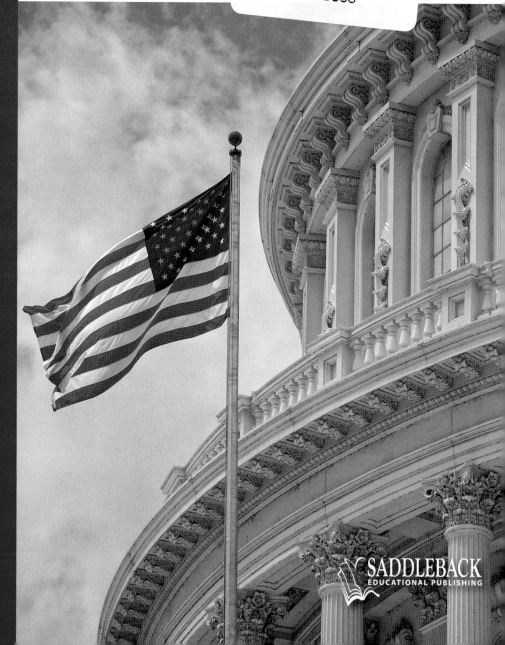

SADDLEBACK
EDUCATIONAL PUBLISHING

SADDLEBACK HANDBOOK SERIES

AMERICAN GOVERNMENT

Foundations
Office of the President
Congress
Supreme Court
Political Parties

Photo credits: page 18: Rena Schild / Shutterstock.com; page 19: Everett Historical / Shutterstock.com; page 22: Joseph Sohm / Shutterstock.com; page 26: Everett Collection Historical / Alamy.com; page 30/31: White House Photo / Alamy.com; page 45: Drop of Light / Shutterstock.com; page 47: Christopher Halloran / Shutterstock.com; page 48: Drop of Light / Shutterstock.com; page 49: Everett Collection Historical / Alamy.com; page 55: Stefano Tinti / Shutterstock.com; page 56/57: txking / Shutterstock.com; page 61: Susan Montgomery / Shutterstock.com; page 67: Everett Collection / Shutterstock.com; page 68: txking / Shutterstock.com; page 70/71: a katz / Shutterstock.com; pag 73: Joseph Sohm / Shutterstock.com; page 77: Everett Collection Historical / Alamy.com; all other images from Shutterstock.com

SADDLEBACK
EDUCATIONAL PUBLISHING
www.sdlback.com

ISBN-13: 978-1-68021-120-7
ISBN-10: 1-68021-120-X
eBook: 978-1-63078-435-5

Printed in Guangzhou, China
NOR/0517/CA21700485

20 19 18 17   2 3 4 5

TABLE OF
CONTENTS

Introduction

Article I of the United States Constitution created Congress. It gave Congress its powers. Set its limits. It is the longest article. There are 10 sections. Each says how Congress works.

Article I, Sections 1–10

1. Gives Congress the power to make laws. Only Congress has this power. Congress has two houses. The House of Representatives is one. The Senate is the other.

2. Creates the rules for the House.

3. Creates the rules for the Senate.

4. Says that states can decide how and when to hold elections and meetings. It says that Congress must meet once a year.

5. Creates the rules for Congress. Each house must have most of its members present to meet. Each house must keep a record of what happens in meetings. It is a journal. Now it is called the *Congressional Record*.

6. Says that members of Congress get paid. They cannot have another job in the government. Not when they are in Congress.

7. Explains how a **bill** becomes law.

8. Names the powers that Congress has. It says Congress can pass laws that it needs to carry out its powers.

9. Names the powers that Congress does not have.

10. Limits the power of the states. They cannot take certain actions. States cannot build an army in times of war. They cannot make their own money.

Congress met for the first time in 1789. It was in New York City. There was a to-do list of jobs. The first job was to elect the president. George Washington won the vote. John Adams won vice president.

Their next job was to raise money. The government needed cash to work. Congress decided to collect taxes. It decided what to tax. Congress passed its first tax law.

Next Congress set up the executive branch. It had three departments. The State Department. It was run by Thomas Jefferson. The War Department. It was run by Henry Knox. And the Treasury Department. It was run by Alexander Hamilton.

Then Congress set up the judicial branch. Congress passed the Judiciary Act of 1789. This created the Supreme Court. It set the size of the court and how it worked. Congress could create lower courts too. Congress named someone to be the head of the Justice Department. This was the attorney general. He gave legal advice to the president.

Finally Congress had to decide on a bill of rights. The Constitution gave people some rights. But the states wanted their rights protected. They wanted the government to have less control. They told James Madison their ideas. He agreed with some of them. He wanted people to have personal freedoms. Their rights should be protected. But he did not want to limit the power of the government. Madison asked to change the Constitution. He wrote the Bill of Rights. It gives people basic freedoms.

The first Congress had 91 members. There were 65 representatives and 26 senators. Of that group, 34 were lawyers. There were also soldiers, farmers, businessmen, teachers, and doctors.

Today Congress has 435 representatives and 100 senators. Of that group, 104 are women. There are 46 African Americans. In fact, the 114th Congress is the most diverse in our nation's history. There are 184 lawyers. Many former governors, state legislators, and mayors also serve.

Power must never be trusted without a check.
—John Adams

Chapter 1
A TRIP TO WASHINGTON

It was 2015. Schools were on spring break. Ginger Netten did not go to Disney World. She did not stay home in Arizona. The 14-year-old was in Washington, D.C. It is our nation's capital.

Ginger took pictures in front of the White House. She saw the Washington Monument. Then she went to Capitol Hill. The U.S. Capitol is there. It's where Congress meets. There are offices and **hearing** rooms. Other office buildings are nearby for workers in Congress.

Ginger went there to talk to members of Congress. She was part of a group. They asked Congress to give scientists $2.06 billion. The money would be used to study diabetes. It is a disease. The body can't make enough insulin. This causes too much sugar in the blood. About 30 million Americans have the disease. Ginger is one of them.

"I have to tell them how hard and difficult it is to live with this disease," Ginger said.

Think About It: *Does a big majority cause big trouble?*

[WHY CONGRESS?]

Why didn't Ginger talk to the president? Or go to the Supreme Court? Each is a part of the U.S. government. Ginger knew how government works. She knew it has three branches. The president runs the executive branch. Its job is to enforce laws. The Supreme Court is part of the judicial branch. Its job is to interpret laws.

Congress has a job too. It is the legislative branch. Congress makes laws. They are the rules people must follow. Congress gets money. It also spends money. Money to build. Money to fight  wars. And it gives money to scientists.

"I have met with senators and congressmen before," Ginger told a reporter. "I know if I put my heart into what I am saying, and make sure they understand where I'm coming from, I know I have done my best ..."

Congress did give money for diabetes research. But it was not as much as Ginger's group had asked for.

HISTORY HAPPENED HERE

Event: American Civil War

Where: Capitol Building

When: September 1862

The U.S. Civil War was bloody. Rebels from the South fought the Union. The Second Battle of Bull Run was fought near Washington, D.C. It was on August 28. Fighting lasted two days.

The Union lost. Soldiers needed a hospital. Beds were set up in the Capitol. Some were under the dome. Others were in hallways. About 1,200 hurt soldiers stayed there until October. The war dragged on. The army also used the Capitol as a bakery. Soldiers lived there too.

[POWER TO THE PEOPLE]

The authors of the Constitution worked hard to create Congress. They wanted it to be the most important part of government. Why? England's King

George III used to rule America. He had too much power. Americans were forced to do things they did not want to do. A revolution began. The goal of the war was to break from the king. To be free. Our nation was born when England lost the war.

The authors, or framers, had to form a new government. They did not want one person to have as much power as a king.

The framers instead created Congress. They gave it powers. One of its jobs was to look out for people. To help them. It was up to Congress to "promote the general welfare" of the nation.

Congress became the "People's Branch." Citizens picked its members. Senators. Congressmen. Each senator represented a state. Each congressman represented a small part of a state. Called a district.

It was a new type of government. It was a republic run by laws. People elect their leaders. They make the decisions, not kings or queens.

[POWER UP]
Congress had a lot of power when the nation was new. Most presidents did not. Some refused to let Congress bully them. Andrew Jackson stood up to Congress. He tried to do away with the national

Andrew Jackson

bank. Congress had set it up. Congress scolded Jackson. The president didn't care. He still changed the banking system.

Ulysses S. Grant

Congress wanted Abraham Lincoln to fire a general. It was during the Civil War. The general was Ulysses S. Grant. Lincoln did not listen. Grant helped win the war.

The power of the president grew over time. By the 1940s, the president became the most important person in government. Congress had less power over time.

[FRUSTRATION NATION]

Congress can be a rough place to work. It can be hard to get things done. It's annoying. Citizens get fed up. So does the president.

Sometimes there is **gridlock**. Nothing gets done. The executive branch may be from one party. The lawmaking branch is from another party. It is hard for them to agree. But the point of a democracy is to work things out. Cooperate. Lawmakers may agree for the common good.

Congress frustrated President John Adams. He did not get along with it. Adams made a joke. "I have come to the conclusion that one useless man is a disgrace, that two become a law firm, and that three or more become a Congress."

FACES IN THE CROWD

Joseph Rainey
Born: June 21, 1832
Died: August 1, 1887

Joseph Rainey had been a slave. He was also the first African American to be in Congress. It was in 1869. That's four years after the U.S. Civil War. Rainey was from South Carolina.

Chapter 2
TWO HOUSES, ONE CONGRESS

What should Congress look like? The framers scratched their heads. One house? Meaning one body that makes laws. Or should there be two houses that make laws? It was a big decision. The framers argued. They fought. At last they came up with the answer. Congress would have two houses. It would be bicameral. There would be a Senate. And a House of Representatives.

The framers were careful to have a balance of power. The smaller states had smaller populations. They were afraid the larger states would rule them. Two houses would give the states equal power. It would prevent tyranny.

[IN THE SENATE]

Each state would have the same number of senators. Two from each state. That made the small states happy. Senators were expected to be wise. They would not let small problems guide their choices.

Senators are elected every six years. One-third of all senators are up for reelection in any given election. A senator has to be at least 30 years old.

Today the Senate is made up of 100 people. Each state has two senators. At first, state legislatures picked each senator. That changed in 1913. Now voters elect them.

[IN THE HOUSE]

Each state's population would decide how many people served in the House. That made the big states happy. The House of Representatives is often called the "People's House."

California is the largest state in the Union. It has 38.8 million people as of 2014. That means it has the most House members. There are 53. Some states have only one member. There are seven. Alaska. North Dakota. South Dakota. Wyoming. Montana. Delaware. Vermont.

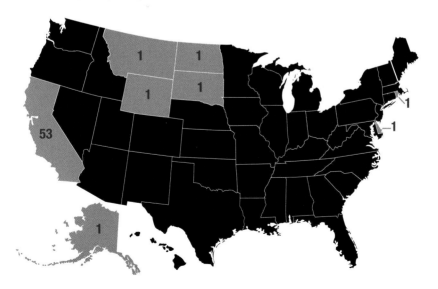

House membership is based on a state's population. The number of members can change. Every 10 years the government counts the U.S. population. This is called a census. The latest one was held in 2010. Many states lost population. People left. So they lost House seats. New York and Ohio lost two. Some states grew. They gained seats. Florida gained two. Texas, four.

The House has 435 members. Each serves a two-year term. Then they are up for reelection. Elections are held in even years. Members of the House must be U.S. citizens for at least seven years. They have to be at least 25 years old. And they must live in their state at the time they are elected.

Each member represents a district. Districts are parts of the state. Some are very small. Those in

New York City are only a few blocks long. Others
are entire states. Some districts are huge. The
21st District in New York is made up of parts of 10
counties.

Other members are not from states. One is from
Washington, D.C. Five are from territories. Guam.
American Samoa. The North Mariana Islands. The
U.S. Virgin Islands. Puerto Rico. Each has a member.
They can discuss issues. Members help set policy.
But they don't have a vote.

UNITED STATES TERRITORIES

The Senate has been called the upper house. The House, the lower house. The first Congress met in 1789. It was in New York City. The Senate's room was one floor above the House's. But both bodies are equal. Each has its own powers. Both must agree on a bill before it can become law.

[THE "GREAT ANCHOR"]

It was January 26, 1830. Two men were talking about land. It would have put most people to sleep. But then the subject changed. It got more interesting. It was about slavery and the role of the government.

Robert Hayne was a senator. He was from South Carolina. It was a Southern slave state. The South's economy was based on slave labor. Hayne stood on the Senate floor. He said the non-slave states in the North were trying to ruin the South. The U.S. was only a group of separate states, he said. States could leave the Union anytime. The states could ignore the will of Congress.

Daniel Webster was a senator from Massachusetts. It was a non-slave state. He sat and listened to Hayne. Then he stood up. Webster spoke. His voice grew loud. He gave Hayne a lecture. It went on for two days.

Daniel Webster

Webster said states could not leave the Union anytime. "Those who administer it are responsible to the people." The people made the government.

His speech became famous. It was the type of speech the framers had in mind. They believed the Senate should be made up of statesmen. People that made wise decisions based on experience.

James Madison helped write the Constitution. He said the Senate was the "great anchor of government."

ON THE JOB

Desks mean a lot in the Senate. Daniel Webster's desk is still there. The senior senator from New Hampshire uses it. It might seem odd. Webster was a senator from Massachusetts. But he was born in New Hampshire.

Senator George Murphy's desk was popular in 1965. He kept candy there. The other senators got to enjoy it. Today the Senate still has a "candy desk." It's in the back of the room.

[WORKER BEES]

Members of Congress have a hard job. But they also have help. Each member is able to have a group of workers. A paid staff. Each member can have up to 18 full-time workers. Some work in Washington. Others work back home. A senator can have dozens of workers. Some work in the senator's home state. Each House and Senate **committee** also has a staff.

The hours are long. The work is hard. The workers do many things. Some write laws. They study issues. Others work with leaders back home. They make sure their boss gets credit when there is a success.

Staff also help people work with government **agencies**. They make sure towns and cities get money for projects. Streetlights. Sidewalks. Parks.

Chapter 3
POWER OF CONGRESS

President Lyndon Johnson needed help. He wanted a bill to become law. It was President Kennedy's civil rights bill. The bill was Johnson's top goal. President Kennedy had been killed. Johnson had to prove himself. He wanted to finish what Kennedy had started.

The bill would make racial discrimination illegal. But it was going nowhere. The House Rules Committee slowed down the bill. Howard Smith ran the committee. He was a congressman.

The committee sets the ground rules for the **debate**. A debate is a formal talk between people. Both give their views. But House members cannot talk forever. There are too many members. Rules are needed. So each member gets a say.

Smith disliked the bill. He wanted to kill it. There would be no House vote. That's what he hoped. Smith wanted the bill to die in committee. House members could not vote. Not if he kept the bill locked up.

Smith added to the bill. He hoped it would die. His committee was talking about Title VII. This was a ban on work discrimination. To the list, Smith added sex. The bill got complicated. There would be no discrimination. Not based on race. Color. Religion. National origin. And now, sex. Smith hoped Title VII would end it. He thought men did not want women to be equal.

Title VII
No Discrimination
Based On

The president put pressure on Smith. He said he would pass around a **petition**. Called a discharge petition. This would avoid Smith. It would release the bill. The House would get to debate. This was rare. Congress didn't like it.

Johnson had many allies in the House. Some of them owed the president a favor. They forced Smith to hold hearings. Take a vote. Release the bill. Let it out of the committee. The House voted. The bill passed. Next it went to the Senate.

Think About It: *The Constitution has an "elastic clause." It says Congress can make any laws that are "necessary and proper." Why is the phrase called "elastic"?*

[PROBLEMS IN THE SENATE]

The civil rights bill was unpopular. Congress didn't like it. Many voters didn't like it either. It was also

in trouble in the Senate. A few senators held a
filibuster. At the time this meant a very long speech.
Senators used it so a bill would not get a vote. It
lasted for months.

A senator wanted to end the speeches. He
wanted senators to vote on a rule. It is called **cloture**.
It means closing debate. Two-thirds of the Senate
needed to agree.

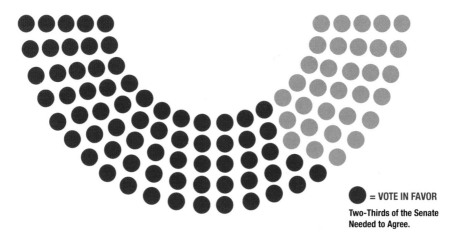

● = VOTE IN FAVOR
Two-Thirds of the Senate
Needed to Agree.

The senator spoke. He talked about why the
speeches needed to end. He said the bill would
help people. It would make them equal. "We have a

firm duty to use the instrument at hand; namely, the cloture rule, to bring about the enactment of a good civil rights bill."

Senators voted. Cloture passed. Debate ended. A vote on the bill was taken. The Civil Rights Act of 1964 became law.

Cloture is Rule 22. It is the only way to stop a filibuster. Filibusters can block or slow down a bill. Rule 22 limits it. Senators can debate only 30 more hours after the rule. As of 1975, three-fifths must vote for cloture. That means 60 senators must agree. Then the filibuster ends.

[BILL CRAZY]

The main job of Congress is to pass laws. Laws start

out as bills. Bills are ideas for new laws. Congress looks at thousands of bills each year.

Some bills are complicated. Like the Affordable Care Act. Others are simple. Like the naming of a post office. In 2013–2014, 3,809 bills were filed in Congress. Only 223 passed.

The power of Congress is spelled out. It is in Article I of the Constitution. Some powers are **specific**.

SPECIFIC POWERS
- Admit new states
- Borrow money
- Collect taxes
- Declare war
- Establish lower federal courts
- Print money
- Propose amendments to the Constitution
- Regulate trade
- Support an army and navy

Congress has some unwritten powers. These are implied powers.

> **IMPLIED POWERS**
> - Draft people into the military
> - Set a federal minimum wage
> - Set up a national bank

[THINGS CONGRESS CANNOT DO]

There are things Congress cannot do. The Constitution does not allow it. It cannot jail a person without a legal reason. It cannot make a law after the fact to justify its actions. Congress cannot take away a person's  rights. Those rights are in the Bill of Rights. They include freedom of speech, religion, press, and others.

Congress sometimes tries to limit these rights. A group of senators got together in 2013. They wanted Congress to decide who should be called a journalist. A journalist is a news reporter. They said only paid reporters should be protected for what they write or say. It did not cover bloggers or others that publish online. People got angry. They said it went against freedom of the press. The idea went away.

[JOINT DECISIONS]

Going to war? Raising taxes? The House and Senate must act as one. Each has to pass the same version of a bill. They have to agree before it becomes law.

President James Madison found out how hard that could be. He wanted to go to war. It was 1812. The British were taking American ships. They were forcing U.S. sailors to work for them. They were also

James Madison

supporting Native Americans to attack faraway villages.

Madison had enough. He sent a "war message" to Congress. It listed all the bad things Britain was doing. The House and Senate both had to agree to go to war. They had to pass a declaration of war. Congress fought for weeks. The vote was close. The House voted 79–49 for war. The Senate voted 19–13.

[SPECIAL POWERS]

Each group has its own special powers. Only the House can propose tax bills. It can also impeach. *Impeach* means to charge a government official with a crime.

The House has impeached two presidents. One was Andrew Johnson. It was in 1868. He was impeached for firing the secretary of war. The House also impeached Bill Clinton. It was in 1999. He was charged for lying under oath in a court case. The House could not remove the men from office. Only the Senate could do that. It had to hold a trial first. The Senate found both presidents not guilty.

ON THE JOB

The government passes laws and rules. To some they seem silly. For example, it is illegal to issue a fake Weather Bureau forecast. One law forces hotels, restaurants, and airlines to let miniature horses be service animals. In 2012, Congress passed a law to get rid of certain lightbulbs. Called incandescent bulbs. It wanted people to start buying energy-saving bulbs.

The Senate has another special job. "Advice and consent." The president has to seek the "advice" of the

Senate. This happens when making **appointments**. The president chooses judges. Ambassadors. Cabinet heads. Senate committees hold hearings on each choice. Then the hearings are over. The entire Senate has to "consent" to each choice. It is also the Senate's job to approve treaties with other nations. The president makes treaties.

The year was 1789. It was the first time the Senate said no to a president. President George Washington's pick was rejected. The president had not asked some senators. Washington was not happy. But he offered another person for the job.

HISTORY HAPPENED HERE

Event: Robert Bork's Nomination to the Supreme Court

Where: U.S. Senate

When: 1987

President Ronald Reagan appointed a Supreme Court justice. He wanted Robert Bork for the job. The Senate Judiciary Committee held hearings on the nomination. It rejected Bork's appointment. The vote was 9–5.

The vote should have ended it. Bork should have withdrawn. However, he wanted the full Senate to vote on his nomination. The Senate voted against him. Reagan had to pick someone else.

Chapter 4
ORGANIZATION OF CONGRESS

Every new Congress begins on January 3. It is also an odd-numbered year. That year follows a general election. A Congress lasts for two years. Each year is a separate session. Session 1 of the 114th Congress began on January 3, 2015. Session 2 will end on January 3, 2017.

There are four House officers. The clerk. The chief administrative officer. The sergeant at arms. And the chaplain. They are elected at the beginning of each Congress. Officers are not House members. They have no political power. House officers from the last Congress continue their jobs. They wait till new officers are elected.

It's the first day of a new Congress. There is no Speaker. The clerk calls the House to order. The chaplain says a prayer. Next is the Pledge of Allegiance. Roll is called. Then the Speaker is elected. The sergeant at arms announces the Speaker's name. Then the new Speaker is led to their chair. The Speaker makes a speech. Then they repeat the oath of office. The Speaker gives the oath to all members.

The political parties state their leaders. They include **majority** and **minority** leaders and whips. Then the House officers are elected. The majority party's candidates usually win.

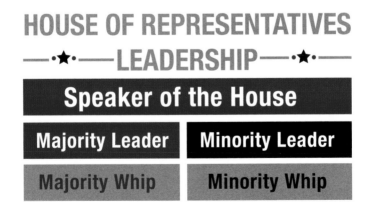

HOUSE OF REPRESENTATIVES
─·★·──LEADERSHIP──·★·─

Speaker of the House

Majority Leader	Minority Leader
Majority Whip	Minority Whip

Finally everything is in place. The majority and minority leaders call the president. Congress is ready to get to work. Rules are decided. Meeting times are agreed upon. The president learns who has been elected Speaker. This is the job of the House clerk.

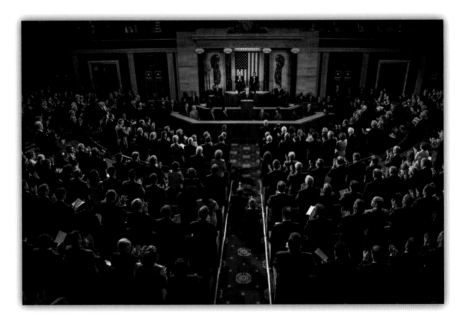

The Senate is ongoing. Only one-third of its members is up for reelection at any one time. It doesn't set up new rules with every new session. The session begins. The vice president bangs the gavel. "Will the Senate come to order," he shouts. Things quiet down. The Senate chaplain says a prayer. Next is the Pledge of Allegiance. The vice president swears in new senators. He poses for pictures with them and their families. The Senate then gets to work.

Think About It: *Longest-serving Speaker Sam Rayburn said leaders must also "know how to follow." Otherwise they cannot lead. Is this a true statement?*

[HOW CONGRESS WORKS]

Political parties decide how Congress works. There are two main parties. Democrat. And Republican. Each has its own ideas.

The Senate has a majority party. So does the House. That is the party with the most members. The Senate has a minority party. So does the House. That is the party with the fewest members.

Each party elects its own leaders. Leaders for the Senate. Leaders for the House. Each party has a special meeting. It happens when each session of Congress begins. These leaders build support. They organize votes. And they make plans.

The Speaker is always a member of the majority party. The Speaker has the most power. Next is the majority leader. That is the second most powerful position. The majority leader helps the Speaker. They plan the party's actions. The minority leader

Paul Ryan, Speaker of the House 2016

has limited power. Why? There are less members in the minority. But there is always the next election. The majority may lose too many seats. The minority leader may become the next Speaker.

The Senate also has majority and minority leaders. A senator runs the Senate's meetings. The senator is usually from the majority party. They have been a senator for a long time. The role is called the president *pro tempore*. That's Latin. It means "for the time being." The president pro tempore takes the place of the vice president. The vice president is rarely present. The job is mostly ceremonial.

Vice President Joe Biden, former Speaker John Boehner, and president of Ukraine, in 2014

[POWERFUL JOB]

The majority party in the House has a big job. Pick a Speaker. The Speaker is a very important job. They run the House's meetings. The Speaker picks who sits on committees. And who runs them. How do House members address the Speaker? They have to say "Mr. Speaker" or "Madam Speaker." The Speaker sets the **agenda**. They decide when a bill can come up for a vote.

Some Speakers have a lot of power. Sam Rayburn was one. He was from Texas. Rayburn worked on his father's farm. Then he ran for Congress. Rayburn was a Democrat in the 1940s. Democrats at the time held power in the House. They had more

Sam Rayburn

members. Rayburn controlled what bills became laws. What issues Congress could look into.

Rayburn was fair. He had many friends. People

did things for him. Things he wanted done. People were loyal. That gave Rayburn more power.

"You cannot lead people by trying to drive them," he once said. "Persuasion and reason are the only ways to lead them. In that way, the Speaker has influence and power in the House."

[WHIPS AND OTHER JOBS]

There are other jobs in the House and Senate. The House has a majority leader. So does the Senate. There are also minority leaders.

The Senate majority leader is powerful. They schedule votes on bills. Pick people to sit on committees. Decide which bills come up for a vote. The majority leader decides which rules the Senate should follow.

SENATE MAJORITY LEADER DUTIES

Schedules Votes

Picks Committees

Selects Bills to Vote On

Chooses Rules to Follow

A Senate rule changed in 2013. The majority leader made the change. Presidential nominations could be brought to a vote by a simple majority. That meant 51 votes rather than 60 votes. This is good if the president's party is the majority party. The president can get nominees approved quickly. This rule does not apply to Supreme Court nominations.

Each party also has a whip. The name comes from foxhunting—"whipper-in." The whip was a worker.

They kept the dogs from straying during the hunt. The whip in Congress sort of does the same thing. They make sure party members vote on important bills. They try to sway people to vote a certain way.

The whip also keeps track of the votes. They count the yes votes. And the no votes. Not every vote is "whipped," however. Only important votes. The whip works with deputy whips. Nine in the House. Eleven in the Senate. The numbers can vary.

The House first used whips. Republicans started it. It was in 1897. The Senate used their first official whip in 1913. This time Democrats were first.

In the House there is a clerk. The clerk of the House. The clerk writes down how each House member voted. The clerk also takes care of the House records. The

ON THE JOB

James K. Polk was the 11th president of the U.S. He served from 1845–1849. He is the only president to also serve as Speaker. He was Speaker from 1835–1839.

House sergeant at arms keeps everyone safe. The sergeant at arms also keeps order.

[COMMITTEE SYSTEM]

Congress has many committees. That's where the real work goes on. These committees see thousands of bills each year. Some are  standing committees. They are permanent. Those committees study bills. They oversee agencies and programs. Like the House Ways and Means Committee. It deals with how to pay for projects. The Agriculture Committee deals with farming issues. The Appropriations Committee deals with money.

Some committees are select. That means special. Their job is to study problems. The Senate has a Special Committee on Aging. It deals with issues involving the elderly.

There are joint committees. One is for the Library of Congress. It oversees the library. It also manages the U.S. Botanical Garden. And takes care of statues in the Capitol. Joint committees have members from both bodies.

Which bills move forward? That is decided by a committee. The committee leader has great influence. They are called chairman. There are 16 standing committees in the Senate. There are 20 in the House.

[POWER TO THE CHAIR]

Committee chairmen have power. Some deal with big issues. They can be as powerful as the Speaker.

One committee is the House Ways and Means Committee. It is the oldest in Congress. It deals with taxes. The committee also writes rules. These rules are for many programs. One is Social Security. Another is Medicare. Dan Rostenkowski was once its chairman. He was one of the most powerful members of the House. He helped pass important laws in the 1980s. Those laws helped retired people. He also helped rewrite the nation's tax laws. After he did that, millions of poor workers did not have to pay taxes.

FACES IN THE CROWD

Nancy Pelosi
Born: March 26, 1940

In 2006, Democrats won a majority. They took control of the House. Nancy Pelosi was named Speaker. The first woman Speaker in history. Pelosi represented California's 12th District. It is in San Francisco. She rose up through the party's ranks. In 2010, she helped with health-care reform. She lost the Speaker's post in 2011. Republicans became the majority party in the House.

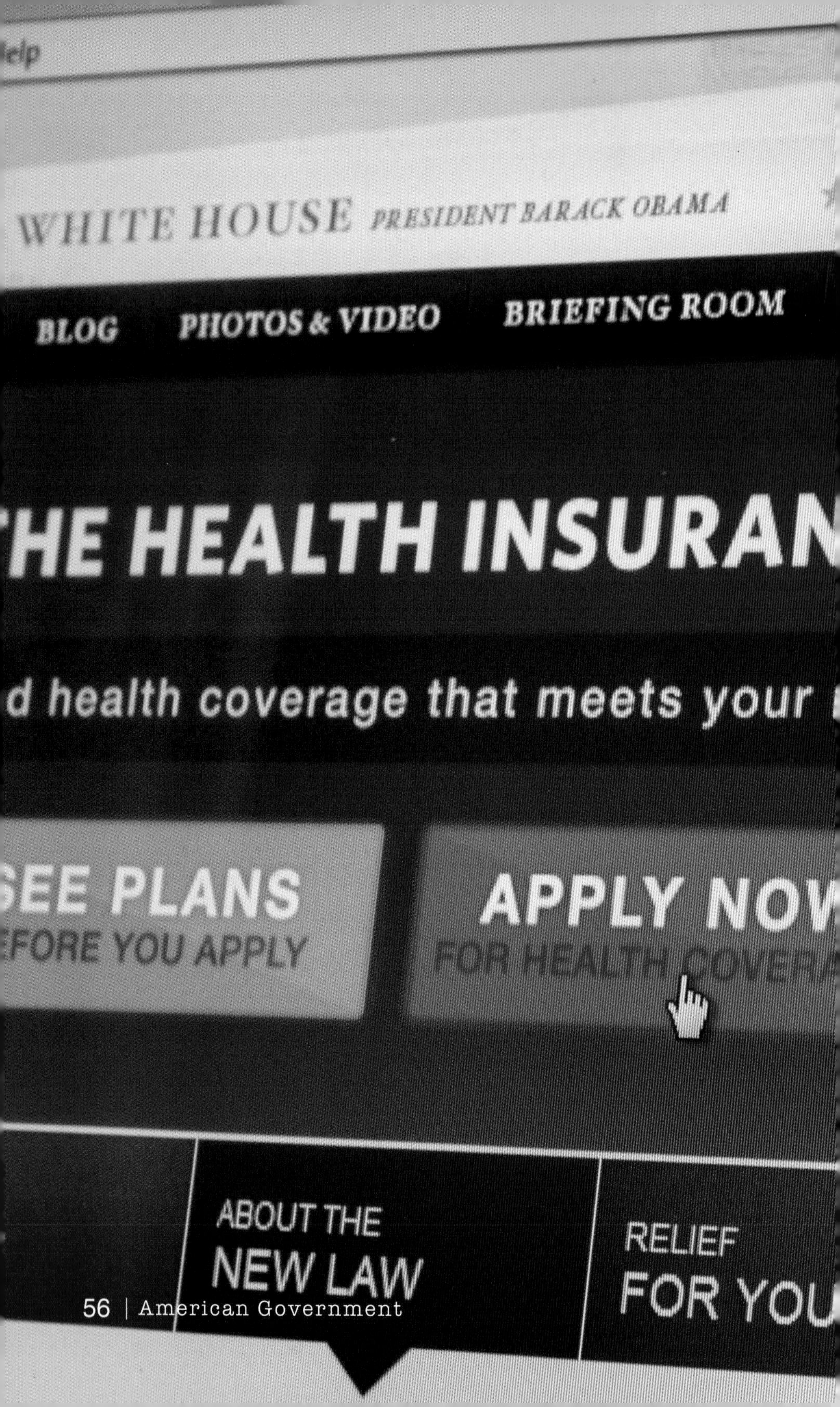

WHITE HOUSE *PRESIDENT BARACK OBAMA*

BLOG   PHOTOS & VIDEO   BRIEFING ROOM

THE HEALTH INSURAN

d health coverage that meets your

SEE PLANS
EFORE YOU APPLY

APPLY NOW
FOR HEALTH COVERA

ABOUT THE
NEW LAW

RELIEF
FOR YOU

Chapter 5
A BILL BECOMES LAW

President Barack Obama sat at a small desk. It was 2010. Nearby were 20 people. Some were members of Congress. One was Marcelas Owens. He was 11 years old. The president took a pen. He signed his name to a bill. The Patient Protection and Affordable Care Act. The bill was now a law.

"Everybody should have some basic security when it comes to their health care," the president said when he signed the bill.

Marcelas's mother did not have health insurance. She had lost her job. Then she couldn't afford it. She became ill and died.

MYTHS
& FACTS

HEALTH C

NEWS

It is hard for a bill to become law. There are many hurdles. Some people did not like the health-care bill. But it made it through Congress. Americans would now have access to health insurance. The government would help pay for it.

"I don't want any other kids to go through the pain that our family has gone through," Marcelas said.

Think About It: *Some bills are controversial. The health-care bill is one. So was Social Security. And Medicare. Do people change their minds about laws they disagree with?*

[GETTING THE BILL]

What is the most important job Congress has? Creating laws. Every law starts out as a bill. A bill has a long trip. It must be approved by the House and Senate. Then the president must sign it.

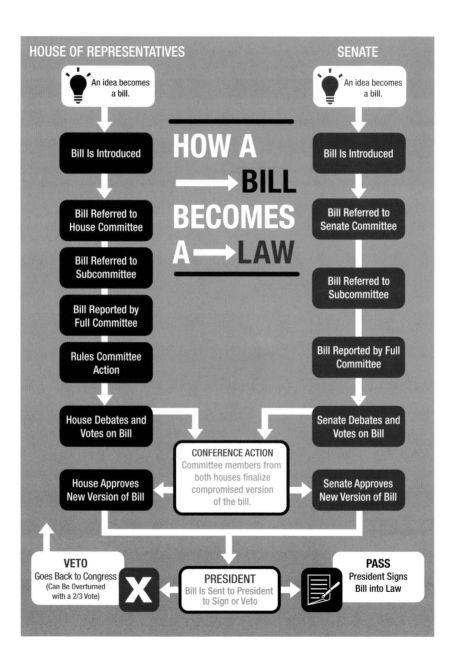

In the House, members may submit a bill. They place it in the "hopper." It is a wooden box. The hopper is near the House clerk. It sits to the side of the clerk's desk. A member must submit the bill. That person is the **sponsor**. The bill's title is recorded. It is printed in the *Congressional Record*. It is the official record of the House and Senate. Then the clerk gives it a number. The Speaker sends the bill to the proper committee.

The *Congressional Record* was first printed in 1873. There are three earlier journals. They cover Congress from 1789–1873. You can read them online.

Every bill starts out as a blank piece of paper. Even the Affordable Care Act. Groups of people spent months meeting. Talking. Researching. Some worked for the president. Others worked for Congress. Some were experts on health care. All worked together. The goal was to change the nation's health-care system. They wanted to open it up to all people. They wrote down what they wanted the bill to say. Finally they were done. The bill was 20,000 pages long.

The bill had to be presented to Congress. The Affordable Care Act's trip would begin in the House. It could have begun in the Senate. Either body is fine. The bill began its journey.

John Dingell

All bills have to be backed by a member of Congress. That someone was John Dingell. Dingell was a congressman. He introduced the health-care bill. It was October 29, 2009.

[COMMITTEE MAZE]

The bill went through many House committees. They

held hearings. Why? Parts of the bill fell under their authority. People testified. They told House members what they thought. Committee members had their say too. They debated.

Bills go through many changes in committee. Any member can change a bill. Each change must be voted on. Yes or no. Changes that pass become part of the bill.

There is a Committee on Rules. It is in the House. All House bills must go through Rules. This committee can control what happens on the House floor. Some rules allow members to change bills. Other rules limit any changes. Sometimes rules say that only certain parts can be talked about. The Rules Committee sets the schedule. It says when a bill will come up for debate.

Bills are read by section on the House floor. Members can ask for changes. They can also debate. Then debate ends. There are three ways to vote. *Viva voce* is a voice vote. Members who vote yes say "aye." Those who vote no say "no." Another way is to stand and be counted. Each side stands. Then is counted as a yes or no vote. There is also an electronic machine. It counts votes.

WAYS TO VOTE

How would the health-care bill be looked at by the full House? The Rules Committee decided. The

Affordable Care Act made its way to the House floor. It was time for a vote. Republicans did not like the bill. But they were the minority party then. Democrats were in the majority. The House voted 220–215. It was approved.

[IN THE SENATE]

The bill wasn't law yet. It had to pass the Senate. Senate committees also held hearings. Senators changed the bill. They added some things. Took other things out.

Senate Democrats were in charge then. They did not want a filibuster. That would stop the bill. Maybe kill it. They used a special rule. Called **reconciliation**.

It said that only 51 votes were needed to pass the bill. It did pass 60–39. One senator did not vote.

But the Senate bill was different from the House bill. That created a problem. Each group has to pass the exact same bill. Only then can it go to the president.

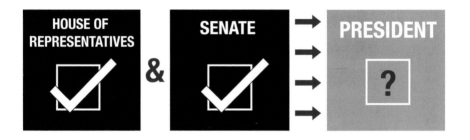

The problems had to be worked out. Usually, Congress sets up a conference committee. That's where members of both groups sit down. They talk about the problems. Then they try to agree.

That didn't happen with the Affordable Care Act. The House agreed to vote on the Senate's version of the bill. It passed. The House vote was 219–212.

Event: Longest Filibuster

Where: U.S. Senate

When: August 28–29, 1957

Members of Congress often try to kill bills they don't like. Take Senator Strom Thurmond. He opposed the Civil Rights Act of 1957. He tried to kill the bill. Thurmond used a filibuster. It was the longest in Senate history. Filibusters were first allowed in 1806. The idea was to give the minority a voice.

Back then a senator had to keep talking. A senator could talk about anything. Thurmond read the Declaration of Independence. He read the voting laws of every state. The senator spoke for a full day. But the filibuster failed. The bill became law.

Senate rules still allow for filibusters. But senators don't have to talk anymore.

[OFF TO THE PRESIDENT]

The health-care bill wasn't law yet. It had one more test. The president had to sign it. Or it wouldn't become a law. Sometimes presidents don't like a bill. Presidents can veto those bills. Reject them. Some presidents have used vetoes a lot. Franklin D. Roosevelt vetoed 635 bills.

Vetoes are part of a system. It is called checks and balances. Vetoes are a way for the president to check the power of Congress. Congress also has a check. It can override a president's veto. It needs a two-thirds vote of each body.

There are two types of presidential vetoes. One is the regular veto. That's when presidents send the bill back to Congress. It is unsigned. Less than 10 days have passed. Congress can override a regular veto. The president can also use a "pocket veto." That's when the president fails to sign a bill. And Congress is not in session. It cannot override a pocket veto.

The president was not going to veto the health-care bill. He wanted it to become law. It was March 23, 2010. President Obama signed the bill.

Barack Obama

"Now it is a fact," said Senator Max Baucus. "Now it is law. Now it is history. Indeed, it's historic."

[DIFFERENT BILLS]

There are four kinds of **legislation**. There is a bill. One is public. It affects the general public. The other is private. It affects a specific person or group.

Joint resolutions are like a bill. They can begin in the House or Senate. The president must approve it before it becomes law.

Then there are **concurrent** resolutions. They do not need the president's signature. These resolutions address the rules of Congress. And express opinions. Both houses must approve. They are not laws.

Simple resolutions usually set the rules for one

body. They are not laws either. Sometimes they are used to make schedules. They may also be used to express feelings, like offering **condolences**.

ON THE JOB

The House and Senate pass the same version of a bill. Next it becomes "enrolled." A clerk prepares the final version. It will be sent to the president. The bill is printed on parchment. The clerk of the House checks it. Makes sure it is accurate. The clerk sends it to the Speaker. The Speaker signs it. Then the Speaker sends it to the president of the Senate. The bill is signed again.

The bill then goes to the White House. The president can do three things. Sign it. This turns the bill into a law. Veto it and return it to Congress within 10 days. Or receive the bill and not sign. If that happens, the bill becomes law. But Congress must be in session. If it takes a break before the 10 days are up, the bill dies.

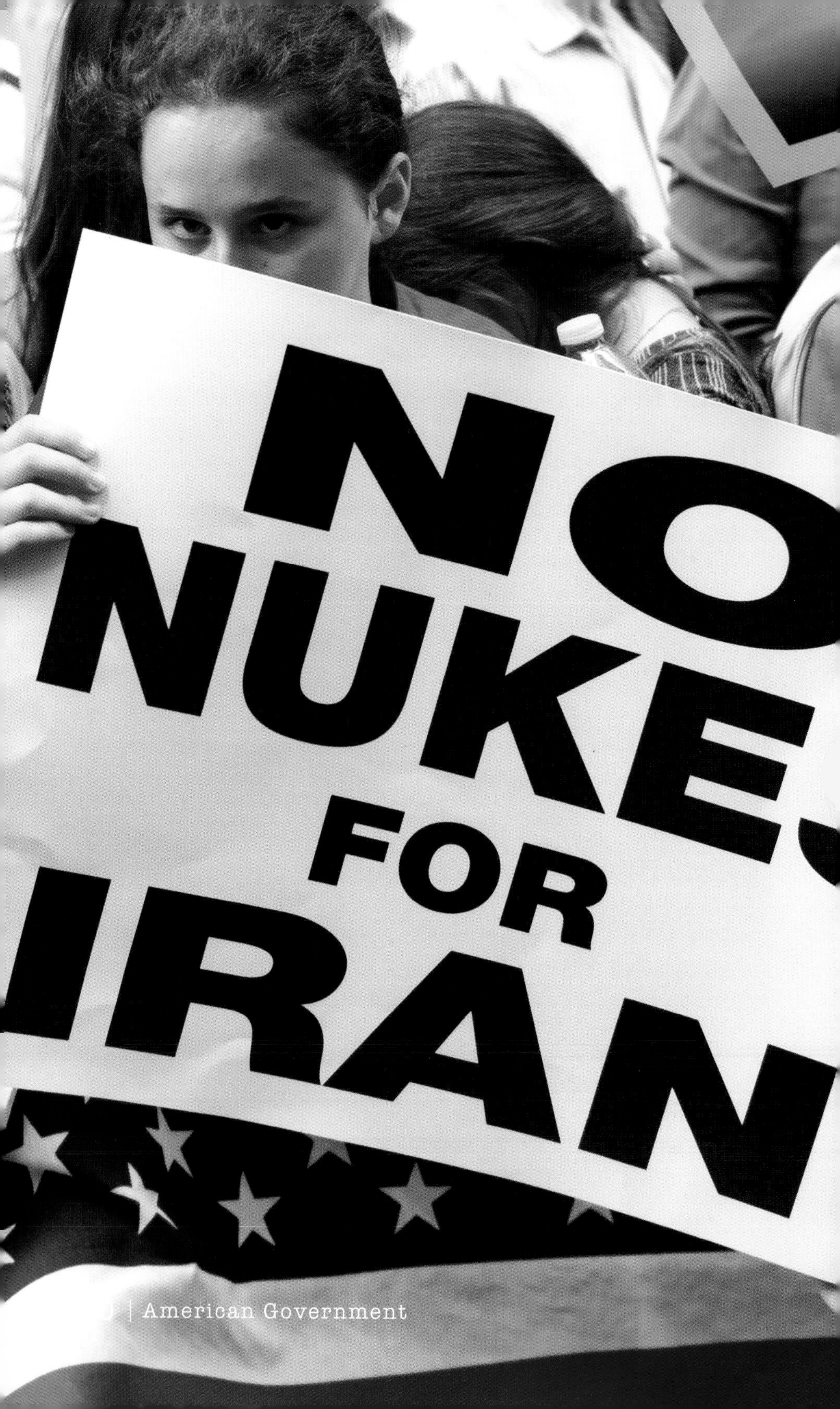
NO
NUKES
FOR
IRAN

Chapter 6
HOW CONGRESS DECIDES

People were talking to Senator Benjamin Cardin. He heard from his rabbi. The voters in his district had something to say. So did his grandkids. All had an opinion. They talked to Cardin about a deal. It was to stop Iran. They wanted to make a nuclear bomb. President Obama helped negotiate the deal. It was with several European nations and Iran. Iran is a country in the Middle East.

The Senate had to vote on the plan. Cardin didn't know what he was going to do. He went home to Maryland. The senator talked to voters. He listened to what they said.

"When Senator Cardin goes to synagogue, he hears about this. When he goes out to dinner, he hears about it. When he sees his grandchildren, he hears about it," a man told a reporter. "It's not that he gets a chance to escape."

Cardin voted against the deal. He didn't think it would stop Iran. They would probably build a nuclear bomb in the future anyway.

Think About It: *"All politics is local." That's what former Speaker Tip O'Neill said. Is this a true statement?*

[VOTERS]

Congress makes many decisions. One way is by talking to voters. A congressman often looks at issues from different points of view. Voters have a point of view. Each congressman has to weigh every issue. They think about what's good for the people. What voters say can change their minds.

Voters have to be kept happy. It's not an easy job. Don't make voters angry. Or they won't reelect their representative. Many senators who voted for the health-care bill were not reelected. Mark Udall from Colorado was not. Neither was Kay Hagan from North Carolina. They lost their jobs. Voters weren't happy with the health-care bill. Other lawmakers simply retired.

[INTEREST GROUPS]

Interest groups also pressure Congress. Interest groups are people that share the same views.

Some represent businesses. Like the Chamber of Commerce. Others want to protect the environment. Like the National Resources Defense Council.

Interest groups talk to Congress. They try to influence policy. Hospitals and nurses have their own special interest groups. They press Congress to pass  laws. Their goal is to keep people healthy.

Lobbyists have a job. They work for special interest groups. It's their job to know the topic. Be experts. Offer evidence. Members of Congress cannot know everything. Sometimes they need help. They use lobbyists to keep them informed.

Money is a tool to many interest groups. Groups help lawmakers get reelected. They buy TV ads. Get voters get to the polls on Election Day.

[PARTY LEADERS]

Party leaders often pressure their members. They want them to vote a

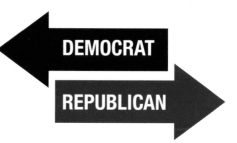

certain way. That can create problems. Party leaders might want a vote to go one way. People back home might want a vote to go another way.

Lawmakers have to think about all this. Balance it out. Going against the party can hurt. A member might not get support for a bill. They might not sit on a popular committee. Programs for their state or district might not get approved. They might not get help so they can get reelected.

[OVERSIGHT DECISIONS]

It was the summer of 1973. There was a hearing. An investigation. It was at the Capitol. Someone had broken into an office. It was for the Democrats. The office was inside a Washington office building. It was called the Watergate.

The break-in happened in 1972. It was a presidential election year. President Richard Nixon was running for reelection. Some burglars had ties to the White House.  Congress thought it should be looked into. A committee decided to see what was going on.

The committee held hearings. Several people testified. Some told Congress the truth about what happened. One was named John Dean. He was a lawyer in the White House. He said people in the executive branch knew about the break-in. The president knew. Dean said the president tried to cover up the crime. The hearings led to Nixon's resignation.

Congress has hearings all the time. They are a way for Congress to look at the actions of the executive branch. It helps lawmakers reach decisions. It's called oversight.

Congress can call people to testify. It can investigate. Try to find the truth. What Congress finds can lead to changes in government. People can be charged with crimes.

Not all hearings are as dramatic as Watergate. Congress uses them to improve government. To decide what programs are not working. To write new laws. And to change old laws.

FACES IN THE CROWD

Joseph McCarthy
Born: November 14, 1908
Died: May 2, 1957

Joseph McCarthy was a senator from Wisconsin. He was a member of a committee. The House Un-American Activities Committee. It was looking for communists in America. In the 1950s the Soviets were powerful. So was Eastern Europe. They were communists. All were enemies of the U.S.

McCarthy said 250 enemies were working in the government. People testified before his committee. McCarthy bullied them. He tried to get people to turn in their friends. The investigation lasted a year. It was called a witch hunt.

In 1954, McCarthy took on the military. People were angry. The hearings went on TV. McCarthy became unpopular. He later lost his power. The hearings ended. The Senate said McCarthy's actions were "inexcusable." "Vulgar." "Insulting."

GAME-CHANGING LAWS

 Securities Act of 1933
First federal rules for the securities industry

 Securities Exchange Act of 1934
Established the Securities and Exchange Commission

 National Labor Relations Act of 1935
Allowed workers to organize unions, engage in bargaining, and go on strike

 The Social Security Act of 1935
Established old-age benefits for workers

 Fair Labor Standards Act of 1938
Established 40-hour workweek, set a minimum wage, and required overtime pay

 Federal Food, Drug and Cosmetic Act of 1938
Established the Food and Drug Administration to make sure food, drugs, and cosmetics are safe

 Federal Aid Highway Act of 1956
Authorized building the U.S. highway system

Civil Rights Act of 1964
Prohibits discrimination based on race, color, religion, sex, or national origin

Social Security Amendments of 1965
Established Medicare and Medicaid

Equal Employment Opportunity Commission Act of 1972
Expanded the Civil Rights Act

Economic Tax Recovery Act of 1981
Reagan-era income tax reform

Personal Responsibility and Work Opportunity Reconciliation Act of 1996
Reformed welfare assistance

Economic Growth and Tax Relief Reconciliation Act of 2001
Bush-era income tax cuts

Patient Protection and Affordable Care Act of 2010
Gives Americans access to affordable health insurance

Congress also looks into issues that can help people. One investigation was after the Gulf War in 1991. Many soldiers got sick. They had a range of illnesses. It was called Gulf War syndrome. Congress looked into it. What Congress found helped many veterans get treatment.

[LAWS HELP ORDINARY PEOPLE]

Legislatures make laws. That means Congress. But citizens can shape laws too. How? They can vote. It is every American's responsibility to vote. Voters share their opinions on Election Day.

Lawmakers can lose their jobs. If people don't agree with them, they won't win the election.

Laws can change people's quality of life. Sometimes one party has a majority. Then they make laws that support their goals. Other times both political parties unite. They make laws for everyone. Those laws help people. Make their lives better.

I've never had time to hate people. I've found that the world will meet you halfway, if you will let it.
—Sam Rayburn, House Speaker (1940–1947, 1949–1953, and 1955–1961)

GLOSSARY

agency: a government department

agenda: a to-do list

appointment: giving a job or position to a person

bill: a proposed law

cloture: closing or limiting debate in the Senate by calling for a vote

committee: a group of people given a particular job

concurrent: something done at the same time

condolences: a feeling or expression of sympathy or sadness

debate: a talk between people in which there is a difference of opinion about a topic

filibuster: an attempt to stop work in Congress by making a long speech

gridlock: a situation in which agreeing on something is not possible

hearing: a meeting in which people testify

legislation: the act of making laws

lobbyist: a person who tries to influence government decisions as it relates to a particular issue, business, or industry

majority: the party that has more members in a group

minority: the party that has fewer members in a group

petition: a formal written request needing a certain number of signatures before it is thought about

reconciliation: trying to make two different ideas exist without conflict

specific: stated exactly

sponsor: the lawmaker most responsible for bringing a bill to the House or Senate

PRIMARY SOURCES
[A LOOK AT THE PAST]

What is a primary source? It is a document. Or a piece of art. Or an artifact. It was created in the past. A primary source can answer questions. It can also lead to more questions. Three primary sources are included in this book. **The Preamble to the U.S. Constitution**. It explains why the framers chose to create a republic. **The Bill of Rights**. It guarantees certain freedoms. And the **Declaration of Independence**. It stresses natural rights. More can be found at the National Archives (online at *archives.gov.*) These sources were written for the people. (That means us.) The people broke free from the king's tyranny. The United States of America was born. Read the primary sources. Be an eyewitness to history.

We the people of the United States, in order to form a more perfect Union, establish justice, insure domestic Tranquility, provide for the common defense, promote the general welfare, and secure the blessings of liberty to ourselves and our posterity, do ordain and establish this Constitution for the United States of America.

[PREAMBLE]

THE U.S. BILL OF RIGHTS

THE PREAMBLE TO THE BILL OF RIGHTS

CONGRESS OF THE UNITED STATES begun and held at the City of New York, Wednesday, March 4, 1789.

THE Conventions of a number of the states, having at the time of their adopting the Constitution, expressed a desire, in order to prevent misconstruction or abuse of its powers, that further declaratory and restrictive clauses should be added: And as extending the ground of public confidence in the government, will best ensure the beneficent ends of its institution.

RESOLVED by the Senate and House of Representatives of the United States of America, in Congress assembled, two-thirds of both Houses concurring, that the following Articles be proposed to the legislatures of the several states, as amendments to the Constitution of the United States, all, or any of which articles, when ratified by three-fourths of the said legislatures, to be valid to all intents and purposes, as part of the said Constitution; viz.

ARTICLES in addition to, and amendment of the Constitution of the United States of America, proposed by Congress, and ratified by the legislatures of the several states, pursuant to the fifth article of the original Constitution.

[BILL OF RIGHTS]

AMENDMENT I

Congress shall make no law respecting an establishment of religion, or prohibiting the free exercise thereof; or abridging the freedom of speech, or of the press; or the right of the people peaceably to assemble, and to petition the government for a redress of grievances.

AMENDMENT II

A well regulated militia, being necessary to the security of a free state, the right of the people to keep and bear arms, shall not be infringed.

AMENDMENT III

No soldier shall, in time of peace be quartered in any house, without the consent of the owner, nor in time of war, but in a manner to be prescribed by law.

AMENDMENT IV

The right of the people to be secure in their persons, houses, papers, and effects, against unreasonable searches and seizures, shall not be violated, and no warrants shall issue, but upon probable cause, supported by oath or affirmation, and particularly describing the place to be searched, and the persons or things to be seized.

AMENDMENT V

No person shall be held to answer for a capital, or otherwise infamous crime, unless on a presentment or indictment of a grand jury, except in cases arising in the land or naval forces, or in the militia, when in actual service in time of war or public danger; nor shall any person be subject for the same offense to be twice put in jeopardy of life or limb; nor shall be compelled in any criminal case to be a witness against himself, nor be deprived of life, liberty, or property, without due process of law; nor shall private property be taken for public use, without just compensation.

AMENDMENT VI

In all criminal prosecutions, the accused shall enjoy the right to a speedy and public trial, by an impartial jury of the state and district wherein the crime shall have been committed, which district shall have been previously ascertained by law, and to be informed of the nature and cause of the accusation; to be confronted with the witnesses against him; to have compulsory process for obtaining witnesses in his favor, and to have the assistance of counsel for his defense.

AMENDMENT VII

In suits at common law, where the value in controversy shall exceed 20 dollars, the right of trial by jury shall be preserved, and no fact tried by a jury, shall be otherwise re-examined in any court of the United States, than according to the rules of the common law.

AMENDMENT VIII

Excessive bail shall not be required, nor excessive fines imposed, nor cruel and unusual punishments inflicted.

AMENDMENT IX

The enumeration in the Constitution, of certain rights, shall not be construed to deny or disparage others retained by the people.

AMENDMENT X

The powers not delegated to the United States by the Constitution, nor prohibited by it to the states, are reserved to the states respectively, or to the people.

IN CONGRESS, JULY 4, 1776.

The unanimous Declaration of the thirteen United States of America,

When in the course of human events, it becomes necessary for one people to dissolve the political bands which have connected them with another, and to assume among the powers of the earth, the separate and equal station to which the laws of nature and of nature's god entitle them, a decent respect to the opinions of mankind requires that they should declare the causes which impel them to the separation.

––

We hold these truths to be self-evident, that all men are created equal, that they are endowed by their Creator with certain unalienable rights, that among these are life, liberty and the pursuit of happiness. That to secure these rights, governments are instituted among men, deriving their just powers from the consent of the governed. That whenever any form of government becomes destructive of these ends, it is the right of the people to alter or to abolish it, and to institute new government, laying its foundation on such principles and organizing its powers in such form, as to them shall seem most likely to effect their safety and happiness. Prudence, indeed, will dictate that governments long established should not be changed for light and transient causes; and accordingly all experience has shown, that mankind are more disposed to suffer, while evils are sufferable, than to right themselves by abolishing the forms to which they are accustomed. But when a long train of abuses and usurpations, pursuing invariably the same object evinces a design to reduce them under absolute despotism, it is their right, it is their duty, to throw off such government, and to provide new guards for their future security. Such has been the patient sufferance of these colonies; and such is now the necessity which constrains them to alter their former systems of government. The history of the present king of Great Britain is a history of repeated injuries and usurpations, all having in direct object the establishment of an absolute tyranny over these states. To prove this, let facts be submitted to a candid world.

He has refused his assent to laws, the most wholesome and necessary for the public good.

He has forbidden his governors to pass laws of immediate and pressing importance, unless suspended in their operation till his assent should be obtained; and when so suspended, he has utterly neglected to attend to them.

He has refused to pass other laws for the accommodation of large districts of people, unless those people would relinquish the right of representation in the legislature, a right inestimable to them and formidable to tyrants only.

He has called together legislative bodies at places unusual, uncomfortable, and distant from the depository of their public records, for the sole purpose of fatiguing them into compliance with his measures.

He has dissolved representative houses repeatedly, for opposing with manly firmness his invasions on the rights of the people.

He has refused for a long time, after such dissolutions, to cause others to be elected; whereby the legislative powers, incapable of annihilation, have returned to the people at large for their exercise; the state remaining in the mean time exposed to all the dangers of invasion from without, and convulsions within.

He has endeavored to prevent the population of these states; for that purpose obstructing the laws for naturalization of foreigners; refusing to pass others to encourage their migrations hither, and raising the conditions of new appropriations of lands.

He has obstructed the administration of justice, by refusing his assent to laws for establishing judiciary powers.

He has made judges dependent on his will alone, for the tenure of their offices, and the amount and payment of their salaries.

He has erected a multitude of new offices, and sent hither swarms of officers to harrass our people, and eat out their substance.

He has kept among us, in times of peace, standing armies without the consent of our legislatures.

He has affected to render the military independent of and superior to the civil power.

He has combined with others to subject us to a jurisdiction foreign to our constitution, and unacknowledged by our laws; giving his assent to their acts of pretended legislation:

For quartering large bodies of armed troops among us;

For protecting them, by a mock trial, from punishment for any murders which they should commit on the inhabitants of these states;

For cutting off our trade with all parts of the world;

For imposing taxes on us without our consent;

For depriving us in many cases, of the benefits of trial by jury;

For transporting us beyond seas to be tried for pretended offenses;

For abolishing the free system of English laws in a neighboring province, establishing therein an arbitrary government, and enlarging its boundaries so as to render it at once an example and fit instrument for introducing the same absolute rule into these colonies;

For taking away our charters, abolishing our most valuable laws, and altering fundamentally the forms of our governments;

For suspending our own legislatures, and declaring themselves invested with power to legislate for us in all cases whatsoever.

He has abdicated government here, by declaring us out of his protection and waging war against us.

He has plundered our seas, ravaged our coasts, burnt our towns, and destroyed the lives of our people.

He is at this time transporting large armies of foreign mercenaries to complete the works of death, desolation and tyranny, already begun with circumstances of cruelty and perfidy scarcely paralleled in the most barbarous ages, and totally unworthy the head of a civilized nation.

He has constrained our fellow citizens taken captive on the high seas to bear arms against their country, to become the executioners of their friends and brethren, or to fall themselves by their hands.

He has excited domestic insurrections amongst us, and has endeavored to bring on the inhabitants of our frontiers, the merciless Indian savages, whose known rule of warfare, is an undistinguished destruction of all ages, sexes and conditions.

In every stage of these oppressions we have petitioned for redress in the most humble terms: our repeated petitions have been answered only by repeated injury. A prince whose character is thus marked by every act which may define a tyrant, is unfit to be the ruler of a free people.

Nor have we been wanting in attentions to our Brittish brethren. We have warned them from time to time of attempts by their legislature to extend an unwarrantable jurisdiction over us. We have reminded them of the circumstances of our emigration and settlement here. We have appealed to their native justice and magnanimity, and we have conjured them by the ties of our common kindred to disavow these usurpations, which, would inevitably interrupt our connections and correspondence. They too have been deaf to the voice of justice and of consanguinity. We must, therefore, acquiesce in the necessity, which denounces our separation, and hold them, as we hold the rest of mankind, enemies in war, in peace friends.

We, therefore, the representatives of the United States of America, in General Congress, assembled, appealing to the Supreme Judge of the world for the rectitude of our intentions, do, in the name, and by authority of the good people of these colonies, solemnly publish and declare, that these united colonies are, and of right ought to be free and independent states; that they are absolved from all allegiance to the British Crown, and that all political connection between them and the state of Great Britain, is and ought to be totally dissolved; and that as free and independent states, they have full power to levy war, conclude peace, contract alliances, establish commerce, and to do all other acts and things which independent states may of right do. And for the support of this declaration, with a firm reliance on the protection of divine providence, we mutually pledge to each other our lives, our fortunes and our sacred honor.

[**DECLARATION OF INDEPENDENCE**]

There are 56 signatures on the Declaration. They appear in six columns.

COLUMN 1

GEORGIA

Button Gwinnett

Lyman Hall

George Walton

COLUMN 2

NORTH CAROLINA

William Hooper

Joseph Hewes

John Penn

SOUTH CAROLINA

Edward Rutledge

Thomas Heyward, Jr.

Thomas Lynch, Jr.

Arthur Middleton

COLUMN 3

MASSACHUSETTS

John Hancock

MARYLAND

Samuel Chase

William Paca

Thomas Stone

Charles Carroll of Carrollton

VIRGINIA

George Wythe

Richard Henry Lee

Thomas Jefferson

Benjamin Harrison

Thomas Nelson, Jr.

Francis Lightfoot Lee

Carter Braxton

[DECLARATION OF INDEPENDENCE]

COLUMN 4

PENNSYLVANIA

Robert Morris

Benjamin Rush

Benjamin Franklin

John Morton

George Clymer

James Smith

George Taylor

James Wilson

George Ross

DELAWARE

Caesar Rodney

George Read

Thomas McKean

COLUMN 5

NEW YORK

William Floyd

Philip Livingston

Francis Lewis

Lewis Morris

NEW JERSEY

Richard Stockton

John Witherspoon

Francis Hopkinson

John Hart

Abraham Clark

COLUMN 6

NEW HAMPSHIRE

Josiah Bartlett

William Whipple

MASSACHUSETTS

Samuel Adams

John Adams

Robert Treat Paine

Elbridge Gerry

RHODE ISLAND

Stephen Hopkins

William Ellery

CONNECTICUT

Roger Sherman

Samuel Huntington

William Williams

Oliver Wolcott

NEW HAMPSHIRE

Matthew Thornton

[DECLARATION OF INDEPENDENCE]

Be an engaged citizen in today's world.
Meet life's challenges after high school. Are
you fully prepared for democratic decision
making? Do you know how to address
and approach issues in a democratic
and responsible way? These five unique
handbooks will show you how.

AMERICAN GOVERNMENT

American Government
FOUNDATIONS
John Perritano

9781680211184

American Government
OFFICE OF THE PRESIDENT
John Perritano

9781680211214

American Government
CONGRESS
John Perritano

9781680211207

American Government
SUPREME COURT
John Perritano

9781680211191

American Government
POLITICAL PARTIES
John Perritano

9781680211221